D0118901

CALGARY PUBLIC LIBRARY

SEP - - 2006

Wolfgang Amadeus Mozart

W. A. Mozart

By Ernst A. Ekker · Illustrated by Doris Eisenburger

NORTH-SOUTH BOOKS · NEW YORK · LONDON

"To be in Vienna is the best entertainment of all," exclaimed Wolfgang Amadeus Mozart to his new wife, Constanze. "Just listen!"

Constanze heard the dull pounding of horses' hooves, whips cracking, screeching, whistling, and children crying. She looked down from the city wall. Cattle were being herded toward the gate below.

Mozart heard the same sounds, but to him, they meant something completely different. He grabbed his pen and reached into his coat pocket where he usually carried some notepaper. Quick as a flash, he scribbled down a melody—not just the tune, but also the tempo, the rhythm, and the instruments necessary to bring this tune to life.

"Did you just see another opera scene?" asked Constanze, smiling.

Mozart nodded.

Constanze laughed. "Now I understand why you hardly ever stop working, and why you even have to write music during a walk on the city wall. All of Vienna is just a big stage for you!"

Mozart laughed, too. "Correct again! I love this stage—almost as much as I love you. After all, I owe my new life to you both."

"You better not love it more than you love me!" warned Constanze. "Or else we'll have a stage fight!"

Just a year before, in 1781, a stage fight had initiated the start of Mozart's new life and it started with a kick.

As a court musician, Wolfgang had been staying in Vienna with his lord and purse-string holder, the Archbishop Colloredo of Salzburg.

When Colloredo suddenly decided to return home to Salzburg, Mozart refused to follow him right away. He had made promising connections on the Viennese music scene, with plans to prepare a concert, as well as to compose new works.

His Salzburger lord became angry with the stubborn subordinate. He insulted him, calling him, "Rascal! Scallywag! Insolent Subject," and telling him that no one had ever served him as poorly as he had. He also threatened to withhold his pay if he didn't return to Salzburg immediately. But Mozart's temper flared up in response, and the fight ended with the archbishop firing him. Soon afterward Count Karl Josef Arco, the chamberlain in charge of all the musicians and servants of the Salzburg court, literally kicked Mozart out of the room.

As much as the boastful and beloved musician complained about this treatment, he was also relieved. At last, he would be free to live as he had always imagined—a life for his music and with his music. Of course, it would be a life with Constanze as well. He felt at home in Vienna: "This bubbling, clamorous, musical city—Vienna—is my city!"

LIKE VIENNA, Salzburg also looked like a stage, set with magnificent scenery. It was in Salzburg, the city of his birth, that Mozart made his first public appearance. When he was only five years old, he appeared in a small comedy—as a *dancer*. Early on, his parents recognized that Wolferl, which was their nickname for him, had music in his blood.

His mother, Anna Maria, came from a musical family in St. Gilgen, on Lake Wolfgang. She remembered how he began to kick in her womb, whenever she would sing an amusing folk song or hum a favorite opera melody. He would even kick when her husband, Leopold, played on his violin, the piano, or the organ.

This passion for movement stayed with Wolferl. The rhythm of a piece of music went straight to his legs, his hands, and through his whole body.

But Wolfgang could also sit still and listen dreamily whenever he heard music, and he heard a lot of it at his home at #9 Getreidegasse, where he was born on January 27, 1756. His father worked as violinist and assistant kapellmeister, or director, of the court orchestra of Archbishop Schrattenbach, Colloredo's predecessor.

His father often practiced at home. He would play music with his friends, and gave piano lessons to his daughter, Maria Anna, who was nicknamed Nannerl. Nannerl was four-and-a-half years older than Wolferl. It was no wonder that three-year-old Wolferl begged to learn to play the piano, and the violin, and the viola, and the organ.

His parents were amazed by their son's miraculous ability. Soon Wolferl played the piano as well as his sister. He could replay melodies after listening to them just one time. He could even play melodies that no one had ever heard before. His fingers magically called forth piano notes that only existed in his mind. He was composing his first music!

Sometimes he would practice an existing piece of music, experimenting with it until it became a completely new piece. He had no idea that his father had plans for him. Father Leo sensed that there was money to be made from this prodigy—perhaps a lot of money. For Wolferl, it was all a game, and a highly amusing one—just as he'd enjoyed learning dances for stage performances. He practiced dancing everywhere—at home in the garden, behind the house, on the cathedral steps, or around one of the many bubbling fountains of the city. He would become completely wrapped up in his dancing, especially when he had an audience, and Nannerl and his parents loved to watch him.

FATHER LEOPOLD saw his children as a miraculous gift from God. He didn't want to keep them at home. "The whole world should see and hear this gift. People will be amazed. And to think that just now, in an age when scholars claim there is an explanation for everything, along comes a miracle like this."

Leopold was already making plans for taking Wolferl on concert tours, and he quickly became a perfect manager. Leopold knew that performances had to be well prepared and that nothing could be left to chance. He also knew that less could go wrong with two child prodigies than with just one, so he created a "Wolferl and Nannerl" show. He posted letters to influential friends and acquaintances in the cities where concerts were planned. Flyers with reports of the children's wonderful piano playing were sent to local newspapers. He even took out paid advertisements. It was clear to him that creative promotion was only half the battle. Leopold, a poorly paid court musician, had to take additional vacation time for each tour, and he had to invest a lot of his own money in the undertaking. He would borrow money from business people in Salzburg for postal coach rides, for room and board in guesthouses, and for clothing and wigs. He even bought a travel-sized piano, which could be used for practicing on the road or for performances in guesthouses.

As an experienced courtier, Leopold knew that although the invitations of kings, princes, or counts brought fame and honor, the big money-making opportunities were at public events—with paid admission.

But no matter how carefully Leopold planned each trip, mishaps would occur. He even ran into trouble when he bought his own carriage for the family to make their travel more comfortable. On one long trip through Germany, France, and then England, a wheel snapped before their first stop.

Luckily, mother had insisted on bringing their servant, Sebastian. He cleverly rigged up a replacement wheel. Although it was smaller than the other three wheels, it worked. Wolferl would never forget this crooked ride, nor would Sebastian, who happened to be a trained barber. This cheerful, helpful servant has been immortalized in one of Mozart's most beloved operas, *The Marriage of Figaro*.

ENGLAND WASN'T FAR AWAY, but logistically, in terms of eighteenth-century travel, it was very far indeed. Eight-year-old Wolferl enjoyed inspecting the boat on the crossing to Dover. After all, he had sailed with this father and sister on a boat on the Danube River from Passau to Linz and on to Vienna just two years earlier.

It didn't take Wolferl long to befriend the crew. When a British sailor greeted him, "Good morning sir! How do you do?" he was amazed when Wolferl fired back in English, "Very well, sir, at your service!"

Wolfgang, who never went to school, had not only learned Italian and French from his father, but some English as well.

His mother worried about him. "Don't walk around on the boat so much—you'll get seasick!" Instead, she was the first one to get seasick. Wolferl was sympathetic, but he had to laugh, for soon all the others were also hanging over the railing.

But the laughter suddenly stuck in his throat when: Yikes! Was that a sea monster rising from the fog? Something was trumpeting and roaring so loudly that Wolferl had to put his hands over his ears. It was just like at home, when the trumpeter Schachtner would come for a visit. The boat's rocking grew worse and worse. The ocean rumbled and grumbled. The fog elephant disappeared, but still the trumpeting could be heard. Was it a storm? A foghorn?

"You are hurting my ears!" scolded Wolferl.

Originally, Wolferl had looked forward to visiting London with his family, but suddenly he didn't feel like going there anymore. To distract himself, he tried to think about something funny. He remembered the New Year's celebration at the French royal court in Versailles a few months before. As a special favor, selected guests of the royal family were allowed to stand and watch the royal family eat. Wolferl was allowed to stand next to the queen and to kiss her hand every now and then. Once she even let him take a bite of her roasted chicken. He almost kissed the chicken and bit her hand!

And later that evening, as a special treat, he was permitted to play the piano for the royal family. He played a four-handed duet with Nannerl. He was allowed to present his first published compositions, brand-new pieces for the viola and piano.

His memories were suddenly interrupted. "Ohhhh . . . I shouldn't have thought about eating," he groaned, as he joined the rest of his family leaning over the railing.

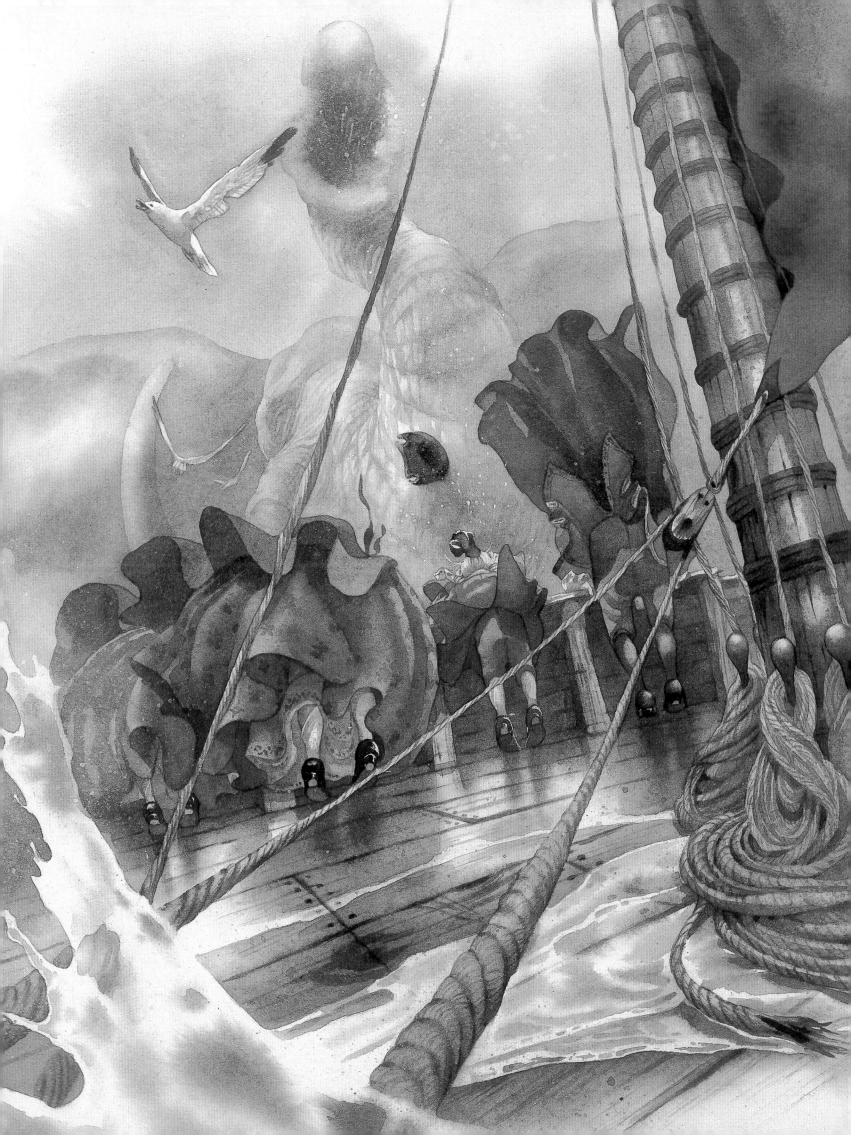

make him laugh with her stories and her cheerful voice. "Remember how everyone wanted autographed pictures of the child prodigies last year? And when father said it was too expensive, you said we should have a whole bunch made and then sell them? And remember father's face when the pictures sold like hotcakes?

"Remember that scientist in London who thought you were a trained monkey? Remember how he studied you? You ignored him and just played the piano as usual, until he finally exclaimed: 'Amazing! This child is a natural!' Then he fainted, while you just crouched on the floor and petted his cat. . . .

"Do you remember how excited father was about the English concert promoters? With their advertising, they succeeded in selling out the halls before we even set foot in London. And remember how stunned your father was: 'A single concert here brings in more than I earn during a year in Salzburg!'"

At last one day, Wolferl said, almost inaudibly: "Do you remember, in London, how our friends thought we were really pious because we went to church as often as possible? And all I really wanted was to practice the organ!"

Anna Maria knew that Wolferl was on the mend. She smiled. "Do you remember how you hopped up and down on an organ during the concert for the royal family? And how the queen remarked, 'That little one is the best organist I know!'" Wolferl tried to laugh. "She must not know many organists!"

Finally, he'd asked for a pen, but he was too weak. So his mother supported his hand as he wrote the score for a new violin sonata he was working on. "At last! The heavens are smiling again," sighed mother Anna Maria with relief.

AFTER LEAVING ENGLAND, the family arrived in The Hague, where they ended up staying far longer than planned. First Nannerl nearly died from typhoid fever and then her brother was struck with the same. Their father watched the money earned during their year-and-a-half in London dwindling away. To Wolferl, it was as if his mother never left his bedside. Throughout the illness, whenever he woke from his feverish dreams, he saw her face and felt her hand stroking him or wiping the sweat from his brow. During lucid moments, he could hear her humming songs from Salzburg or little melodies that Wolferl had composed.

He felt so tired that he couldn't imagine ever waking up again. But she persisted in trying to

SOON AFTER, Father Leopold traveled with his family to Vienna for a big wedding. Empress Maria Theresa's sixteen-year-old daughter was to marry the King of Naples. "And where there is marriage, there are festivities. We will be needed. Maybe Wolferl will be allowed to compose something for the bride and groom."

When a smallpox epidemic broke out in Vienna, everything changed. The bride-to-be died from the deadly disease.

The Mozart family fled Vienna to stay with friends in Olomouc, Moravia (now in the Czech Republic), but even so, they weren't safe. Soon after their arrival, Wolferl was stricken with smallpox. And shortly thereafter, so was Nannerl.

Mother had to be a nurse again. It was so hard on her physically that she lost about twenty pounds. Father Leopold helped as much as he could during the day, whenever he didn't have to attend to urgent business. In the end, the Mozart family was very lucky compared to the emperor's family. Both of the Mozart children survived the outbreak.

As soon as Wolferl was better, Father Leopold was already busy praising the new "miracle" wherever he went. "God has *big* things in store for our son. That's why he was spared," he would proclaim. Many people thought such statements were boastful. Others sensed a clever promotional scheme.

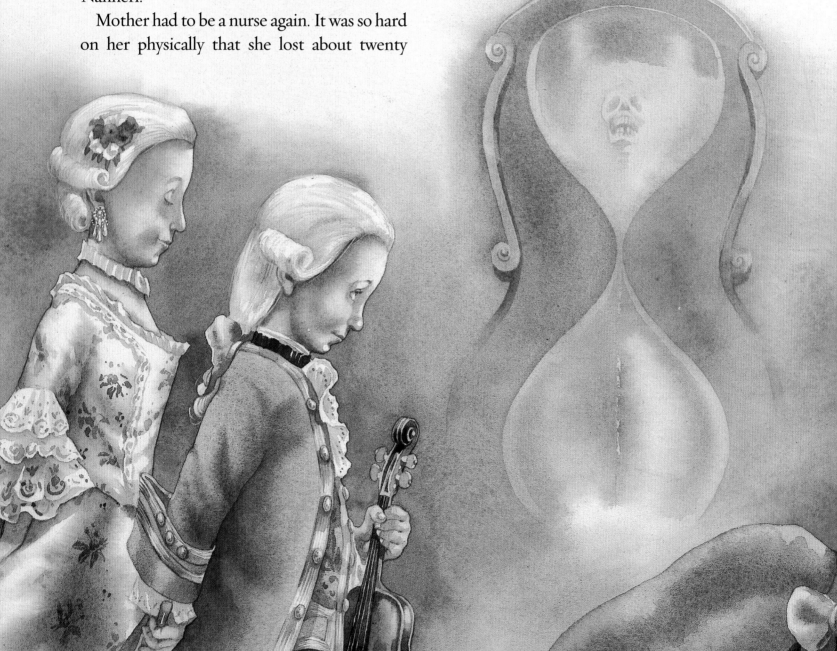

Father Leopold was probably hoping that the new miracle would bring an imperial commission for his son. After all, word spread quickly in Vienna.

When the Mozart family visited the palace and was admitted to the mourning audience, Wolferl felt an icy breeze. The empress sat like a stone on her throne. Father was dismissed the moment he had mumbled his condolences.

Then Maria Theresa looked at Mother Anna Maria. She paused, and waved her over.

Suddenly, the boy had a lump in his throat. He saw his mother, looking at the other mother. She didn't need to say a word. The mothers understood one another without any words, and the empress gently stroked his mother's cheek.

Now Father Leopold expected more than ever from his son, "his gift from God." He was never satisfied with what his prodigy accomplished. He knew he was in a race against time. "Who knows how much longer Wolfgang's fame will last?"

He was right about the race, but in a completely different sense. His son would die at age thirty-five. Despite this, his name—and his music—would live on for hundreds of years.

CARA SORELLA MIA! *My dearest sister! Today Vesuvius is smoking heavily. Whoooosh!* Wolfgang strolled with his father through the old Roman city of Pompeii. Extinguished years ago by a flood of lava, it had just recently begun to be excavated. To Wolfgang, the Pompeiian ruins were like giant stage sets. And the smoke from Vesuvius became comedy masks.

Wolfgang had wanted to write an opera ever since he had first heard one as a six-year-old at Munich's carnival. At a young age, he'd started to compose arias, songs for the singers he'd met on his many travels. They were all delighted to have a piece dedicated to them by the world-famous child prodigy. But what he really wanted to do was to compose an opera that would be sung by children.

As he toured Europe, he would attend operas whenever he could. He loved the serious but ceremonial court music (*opera seria*), as much as the musical comedies (*opera buffa*). In order to unlock the secrets of opera, he studied the scores (the books in which all the notes of the songs and music are written), and he studied many librettos (a libretto is the text of an opera).

Italy is the land of opera. Italian operas are performed all over the world—from Vienna to Paris to London to New York City.

Father Leopold would take many long trips to Italy with his son. Nannerl was upset because she wasn't allowed to come along. But she was no longer a child prodigy—she'd become an eighteen-year-old woman. As a consolation, Wolferl wrote her lots of funny letters:

Yesterday, we went to the opera in Naples. The opera house there is gorgeous. But the king is a typical, rude Neapolitan. At the opera, he stands on a stool so that he looks taller than his wife, the queen. Compared to the king, the queen is pretty and polite. She must have greeted me about six times in the friendliest way.

At fourteen, the boy who had played his "masterpieces" all over Europe for many years no longer attracted massive audiences.

Yet Wolfgang Amadeo (as he called himself in Italy) was still very much a wonder as a composer. Only a few people realized this, and one of those was the famous composer Joseph Haydn.

Father Leopold had wanted his son to make his fortune in Italy, just as Johann Christian Bach (Johann Sebastian Bach's youngest son) had. This German was beloved in England as an "Italian" composer.

In some ways, Father Leopold's plan appeared to work. The name Mozart became well known in Italian music circles. Now Wolferl was acclaimed for his musical compositions, just as he'd been earlier acclaimed for being a child prodigy.

The best Italian musicians would perform his music. Three of his operas premiered in Milan, to great success.

Still, none of this led to his father's dream of lasting fortune. Wolfgang's operas weren't widely performed, and the success didn't last.

Father Leopold considered the time in Italy a huge waste. Why does everything always go wrong? he wondered.

HOME AGAIN, Salzburg felt very claustrophobic to the young musician. "There isn't even an opera house here," Mozart complained.

Ever since he was fourteen-years-old, Wolfgang had worked as concertmaster in the archbishop's court. For the first three years, he wasn't even paid. His father also worked for the spiritual prince. He was the court composer, and as such, his salary didn't stretch very far. One good thing about the job was that the father and son would receive generous vacations, which they used for their journeys. But suddenly, this all ended. Colloredo forbid any more tours. Perhaps he already suspected what Father Leopold had in store for his son: he wanted him to apply for a well-paid position as a court composer for another prince. As such,

he could go to Munich or to Mannheim (which had the best orchestra of all Europe at the time) or perhaps even to Paris. "Marie Antoinette, the young queen of France, knows you, Wolferl. Don't you remember playing with her in Vienna at the emperor's court? Audition for her. Be confident, but not arrogant."

So Wolfgang looked for work in Munich, Mannheim, and Paris. But no one seemed to need a new court composer. He wasn't even admitted to see Marie Antoinette.

Wolfgang wasn't too unhappy about any of this. He used his free time to compose. And he also used it to meet young people. Wolfgang was starved for friends.

When Wolfgang heard that Johann Christian Bach was staying in Paris, he visited him, but

was disappointed. Years ago, in London, Johann had chatted affectionately with him and had given him tips on composing.

Wolfgang got an even bigger shock when he was supposed to give a concert at the home of a Parisian count. First he had to wait a long time to be admitted, and when he got in, the salon was unheated and the piano needed tuning. At last the lady of the house appeared, and when Mozart complained of the treatment, she laughed. Then she gave him a signal to begin playing. Mozart began to perform and soon lost himself in the world of his music. And when he glanced up, he froze. The audience had spread out enormous sketchpads and was drawing! No one was paying any attention to him at all. No one was listening to his music. The composer realized he might as well be playing for the chairs and walls! He jumped up angrily, ready to leave the room, when all at once he saw the audience for what they really were, and he felt sorry for them. He sat down and kept playing. "Maybe the chairs and the walls are listening," he thought.

Shortly thereafter, he returned to the service of the Archbishop of Salzburg, where he would remain for a number of years. His father had called him home. He had begun to think his son was incapable of success. In reality, the works his son had composed during the trip, such as the *Parisian Symphony*, would become immortal classics.

MOZART HAD A STRANGE DREAM. He saw the path of a life—his life. He gazed at the people as he cheerfully hopped from lap to lap. What a lot of laps I've sat on, he wondered.

First was his mother's, whose life was endangered at his birth. She bore seven children in eight years, but only he and Nannerl survived. Still, she sang jauntily:

> *Hello, hello, pointy nose,*
> *Knaller, baller, who goes there?*
> *Bagateller, bagatofferl, it's my Wolferl!*

As long as she sang, he was stuck on her lap. But then suddenly, he landed on his father's knees! All the things that other children learned in school, Wolfgang learned from his father—and so much more. Of course, of everything his father taught him, the most important was composing.

After a while, Wolferl wanted to hop off and play, but his father held him tight, reciting his names like a spell: "Johannes Chrysostomus Wolfgangus Theophilus! Theophilus Amadeo Amadé Amadeus! Loved by God, beloved by God."

When he hopped onto Empress Maria Theresa's lap, she wouldn't let him go either and petted him as if he were her child. She cooed in a silky voice: "Schlumba tumbla kiss kiss kiss! Stri-o stru-o kiss kiss kiss!"

At first he enjoyed all this attention, but then he thought, Even the most beautiful imperial voice can get on your nerves! At that moment, the voice transformed into princely garments, which fit Wolferl like a glove. As much as he tried, he couldn't get out of the clothes, which actually belonged to Max, the empress's youngest son.

Luckily, he landed next on the lap of Johann Christian Bach. They were seated at a grand piano. Twenty fingers raced over the keys, and the keys rang out in jubilation.

Bach's fingers couldn't stop—nor could Mozart's—as they kept conjuring up new melodies from the instrument. Mozart's fingers immediately found notes to accompany the Bach piece. "Listen my lungs, my liver, my stomach too—look at what we dare to do!"

Suddenly Mozart was horrified. "Haven't we already played all of this? No, not once, but often! I do not want to have to hear the same thing forever!"

Prince Colloredo's voice thundered threateningly in his ears. And Mozart thought, I do not want to have to do the same thing forever!

He inhaled deeply and prepared to jump. Already, he was high over the mighty, princely shadow and over the magnificent city of Salzburg, which took his breath away. He flew past his father, who spread his arms as if to catch him. "Hey, hey, hey, they say, one child prodigy hops away!" shouted Mozart joyously.

He would have loved to see the scenes that followed, but his life thread disappeared into a fog. Mozart thought, Oh, I wish I were, if only God wanted, I would be . . . I would be . . .

"What are you mumbling about?" he heard his wife, Constanze, ask from the depths of his dream.

"I *am!*" said Mozart, and woke up.

"I am, what?" asked Constanze.

"I am *yours*," he laughed. And he showered her with kisses.

THERE WAS ALWAYS a lot of dancing in Vienna, especially at carnival time. Wolfgang loved to dance boisterously, often into the early morning hours, and Constanze was an enthusiastic dancer too.

At last, he had friends in Vienna. Working exhausted him. He didn't work mechanically, strictly following the composition rules he had mastered long ago. Instead, he shaped what he'd learned into something new, which flowed out from deep within him. He viewed this particular inexplicable ability as his gift from God. But his gift also drained him. It was no wonder, that after completing a large work, Mozart often threw himself into complete pleasure. He went to plays and operas and masked balls. He had conversations with people who were close to him or with complete strangers. Many of his experiences would later flow back into his work—especially into his operas.

In any case, his first attempt at settling in Vienna was successful. Mozart lived in grand style, with an expensive apartment in the city and servants, despite the fact that he wasn't working anywhere. He supported himself and Constanze by working as a freelance composer for a variety of clients.

Soon he earned many times what his father made at the court in Salzburg.

Of course Mozart didn't just have friends in Vienna—he also had competitors. Antonio Salieri, court Kapellmeister and composer, six years older than Mozart, wrote little other than operas—Italian operas. The two musicians would sometimes play together.

But then the emperor commissioned Mozart to write a German opera, *The Abduction from the Seraglio*. This musical comedy was so well received by Viennese audiences that people would dance to the melodies! Because of his success, Mozart anticipated that he would be asked to write another court opera. But he'd wait four more years before the emperor would ask him to write another opera. This time, it would be an Italian opera, *The Marriage of Figaro*.

The delay was probably because Emperor Joseph II had many other things on his mind besides music. He had big plans to completely reorganize his empire, but he wasn't getting much public support. Rumors flew at the ball. "Who is responsible for your long opera pause?" whispered a Mozart fan to *Figaro*'s composer. "I'll tell you who, it's the jealous, powerful, conceited Salieri!" said Mozart, preferring to blame his competitor for the long wait.

MOZART ONLY HAD TO HEAR TALK of an opera or hear actor's voices, and he'd be beside himself with excitement. Wolfgang Amadeus was born for musical theater. He didn't just think in terms of music, but also in pictures. He'd see the scenery unfold while he was composing the music. And he was known for his temper. Heaven forbid a rehearsal didn't run the way that he wanted. On occasion, he was known to jump from the stage into the orchestra pit to yank an instrument from the hands of a violinist who had been playing the notes incorrectly and to demonstrate the way it was supposed to sound. In Prague's Stände Theater, he wrung his hands in despair as his *Don Giovanni* was being rehearsed. The singer playing Donna Elvira stared unemotionally at the monument to the dead commander—even though the stone statue was supposed to come suddenly to life.

"You have to *scream* in horror," shouted Mozart.

"I cannot scream, I can only sing," she answered.

"Nonsense! Everyone screams when they're frightened," insisted Mozart. The scene was repeated, but the singer continued to stand unemotionally in front of the statue. Exasperated, during the next take, Mozart snuck up behind his Elvira and gave her a good pinch. She jumped and screamed. Mozart was delighted. "Superb!"

Many singers and musicians would not work with Mozart because he was so demanding. Of course, he didn't demand any more from them than he demanded from himself. His wife was used to Mozart being so completely absorbed in his work that he would be oblivious to everything around him. As a child, every noise, even beautiful trumpet music, had bothered his ears. Now he was able to focus so intently that he could continue to compose even in the midst of the ruckus of his large Viennese city apartment, with servants arguing, his youngest child howling, a composition student hammering away at a piano, a voice student singing shrilly, and Constanze giving him an important message, all at the same time.

Mozart worked and worked, but no one could tell he was working. Every aspect of his music developed first in his head. Not only did he come up with the melodies, but also every last detail of the score. When he was finally ready to put the new piece on paper, he'd write it out, fast as lightning. Meanwhile, he'd still be conversing with Constanze. Not even the most shrilly screaming student could distract him.

The people of Prague embraced Mozart and his music. They were much more devoted than Viennese audiences, who accused him of staggering from one sensation to the next. Mozart had numerous popular singers to thank for the fact that all of Prague seemed stricken with Mozart-fever—many locals claimed to know *The Abduction* and *Figaro* almost by heart— but a *real* Figaro was also responsible. The Mozart family's former servant, Sebastian, worked for Prince Fürstenberg in Donaueschingen and had endlessly promoted Mozart's name at court. Now one of Prince Fürstenberg's daughters lived in Prague. Her musical valet—a friend of Sebastian's—was largely responsible for helping to promote Mozart in Prague.

ONE DAY, yet another travel carriage awaited Mozart at the break of dawn. His wife, his friends, and his dog, Gaukerl, were already inside, and everyone was in good spirits. "Away, away to Prague! To your favorite city!" exclaimed Constanze. But Wolfgang Amadeus stood frozen like a statue on the street. "He must be composing again," she thought. And then she shuddered. There was a strange figure behind her husband. Wolfgang Amadeus jumped as he felt a hand on his shoulder. Surprised, he turned around and for a moment thought he'd seen the grim reaper before him, calling him on his final journey. But then he had to laugh at himself. He recognized the messenger and realized immediately what he wanted. His name was Mr. Leitgeb, and he was the steward of Count Wallsegg-Sutpach, from the Goggnitz region. A few weeks ago, the count had requested that Mozart write him a requiem (a mass for the dead). He had already sent a payment and a most unusual contract. Mozart would receive another payment upon delivery of the piece, but he must deliver the original and he would not be allowed to make any copies.

Was the count a collector of famous hand-writings? Or did he want to pass off the requiem as his own composition? It didn't matter. Mozart needed the money and was eager to uphold the contract. But first he had to work on stalling the messenger, as the requiem wasn't even halfway finished.

In the coach, Wolfgang Amadeus sat very still, lost in gloomy thoughts. Constanze was afraid that this sinister stranger had made him uneasy about the trip. She tried her best to cheer him up. Their friends joined in as well, sharing the latest gossip about Joseph II. But Mozart continued to work on "Last Judgment" ("Dies irae") for the requiem. Although personally, he wasn't afraid of death, somehow, he had a mental block about this particular work about the "day of wrath, punishment, and tears." To Mozart, death was a friend who would bring rest and lead him toward the light.

The music in Mozart's head was drowned out by the chatter of his companions. "So Countess Pallavicini met Countess Kinsky and said so loudly that the emperor overheard her: 'Dearest, aren't we poor enough? Our highness, his Majesty, gives the common folk all sorts of parks: the Prater and the Augarten, and possibly also the park at Schönbrunn! But for us, there is no little spot in which we can mingle, undisturbed, among our equals.'

"At this, the emperor turned around, saying: 'If I wanted to be undisturbed among my equals, then I would have to take a walk in the Capuchin Crypt!'"

Mozart couldn't help laughing. He wasn't even angry that his latest work on "Last Judgment" had been wiped from his mind. The music will come back when the time is right, he told himself.

"MY MUSIC IS ME," claimed Mozart. Many people found his claim pretentious. Yet, when he was thirty-one, Joseph II honored him with the title Imperial Royal Chamber Composer. He finally had the position that his father, Leopold, had wanted for him so many years ago. Sadly, his father had recently died before seeing his dream come true.

Despite the title and the fixed salary, Wolfgang Amadeus was still allowed to freelance. The only requirement was that he deliver the dance music in time for the imperial masked balls. Soon people would dance to melodies from Mozart operas again—this time from *The Magic Flute*. Theater director and comedian, Emanuel Schikaneder, had requested this opera for his stage and wrote the libretto himself. The fairy tale of the comical bird catcher, Papageno, and the helpless Prince Tamino who wants to free an abducted princess, even though he is afraid of monsters, was a huge hit with audiences and quickly became a lasting success. Perhaps it was because this opera was full of surprises. From the Queen of the Night to the abductor Sarastro and Papagena the crone, no one is who they initially appear to be, either to the prince or to Papageno or to the audience. Little by little, the prince loses his prejudices, and together with Princess Pamina, he faces difficult trials. They persevere, vowing to create a better world, a world free of hate and violence and full of love.

Mozart sensed that he had achieved something extraordinary with *The Magic Flute*. Because it fell into a middle ground between works that were too challenging and works that were too simplistic, it had wide appeal And the music was brilliant, pleasing to the ears, yet right on target for the story.

During his lifetime, people tried to control Mozart like a puppet—from his father to Archbishop Colloredo to theater directors, musicians, singers, and prima donnas. Today Mozart lives on in his music, 250 years after his birth. The versatility of Wolfgang Amadeus Mozart is amazing. No other composer has been so completely comfortable in a variety of musical genres, from symphonies to chamber music, sacred music to solo music, songs, and opera. His *Magic Flute* is the most frequently performed opera in the world. And even today, his compositions offer a challenge to conductors, musicians, and directors, who constantly discover new things in his music. His music remains full of secrets—and full of Mozart.

1756 Born at 8 P.M. in Salzburg, Austria, on January 27. His mother, Anna Maria, née Pertl, was from a poor civil servant's family in St. Gilgen, Austria. His father, Leopold, was the son of a bookbinder from Augsburg, Austria. Leopold worked as a violinist, music teacher, and composer. From 1743 until his death, he was a court musician for the prince-archbishops of Salzburg.

The Seven Years War between Prussia and Hungary begins. Salzburg did not belong to the enormous Hapsburg Empire at this time, but supported Empress Maria Theresa.

1761 Five-year-old Wolfgang composes his first minuet.

1762 First concert tour to Munich and Vienna. Performance in the Schönbrunn Palace on October 13.

Father Leopold buys his own carriage.

1763–1766 Grand tour of Western Europe.

1767 The prodigy's first theater compositions.

Tour of Vienna, Austria, and Brno and Olomouc (both cities in the current Czech Republic).

Smallpox epidemic in Vienna and other European cities.

1768 First imperial commission for a large mass (*Waisenhausmesse*).

Commissioned by Viennese psychiatrist Franz Mesmer (who developed the theory of animal magnetism) to compose and perform *Bastien und Bastienne*.

1769 Appointed *Third Concert Master*—an unpaid position—at Archbishop von Schrattenbach's court in Salzburg. Until 1773, attended several concert and study tours throughout Italy. Opera commissions in Milan.

1770 In Rome, he was honored by the Pope with the "Order of the Golden Spur."

1771 Death of Archbishop von Schrattenbach.

1772 Count Colloredo, a bureaucrat, assumes the position of Archbishop of Salzburg.

1773 The family moves to a larger home in Salzburg (Tanzmeisterhaus).

1774 Mozart's (first) dismissal by Colloredo.

Tour of Germany with his mother. Meets the Weber family in Mannheim. Helps the young soprano, Aloysia (with whom he was in love), launch her career. (Five

years later, he married her sister, Constanze.) Composer Carl Maria von Weber, one of Constanze's cousins, is born in 1786.

Following the death of the childless Elector of Bavaria, several German states (including Austria) enter the War of the Bavarian Succession (also called the Potato War), which continued until 1779.

1778 The family's journey continues to Paris. Mozart's mother becomes seriously ill. For a long time, she doesn't permit anyone to call a doctor—probably out of frugality. She dies on July 3 and is buried in Paris.

1779 Mozart returns to services as court organist and *Konzertmeister* in Salzburg.

1780 Opera commission in Munich.

Death of Empress Maria Theresa. Her son and co-regent, Joseph II, becomes sole ruler of Austria. He implements important reforms like religious freedom, abolishment of serfdom, and bans grandiose burials.

1781 Mozart's Viennese period as a freelance artist begins.

1782 *Abduction from the Seraglio*. Marriage to Constanze. During nine years of marriage, she gave birth to six children, but only two survived.

1784 Acceptance into the Freemasons, whose ideas influence his compositions (especially his operas).

1785 Mozart's father visits Vienna and also becomes a Freemason, as does Joseph Haydn.

1786 Opera buffa *Le nozze di Figaro* (The Marriage of Figaro).

1787 Travels to Prague: *Don Giovanni*.

Death of his father on May 28.

1788–1790 *Despite favorable economic relations with the Ottoman Empire, there is another war against the Turks (mutual assistance pact with Russia). Emperor Joseph II becomes ill during the campaign and dies in 1790. His younger brother, Leopold II, succeeds him on the throne.*

1791 Trip to Prague.

Premiere of *The Magic Flute* in Vienna (September 30).

Wolfgang Amadeus Mozart dies on December 5. Per Constanze's request, his *Requiem* is completed by his student Franz Xavier Süssmayr.

The publisher thanks Ken Waldherr for his review and support.

Copyright © 2005 by Annette Betz Verlag im Verlag Carl Ueberreuter, Vienna, Munich.
First published in Austria under the title *W. A. Mozart: Ein musikalisches Bilderbuch*
New English translation copyright © 2006 by North-South Books Inc., New York

All rights reserved. No part of this book may be reproduced or utilized in any form or by any means,
electronic or mechanical, including photocopying, recording, or any information storage
and retrieval system, without permission in writing from the publisher.

First published in the United States, Great Britain, Canada, Australia, and New Zealand in 2006
by North-South Books, an imprint of NordSüd Verlag AG, Gossau Zürich, Switzerland.

Library of Congress Cataloging-in-Publication Data is available.
A CIP catalogue record for this book is available from The British Library.

ISBN-13: 978-0-7358-2056-2
ISBN-10: 0-7358-2056-2
1 3 5 7 9 10 8 6 4 2
Printed in Belgium

*Now that you've spent some time with Wolfgang Amadeus Mozart and have gotten to know his world,
we suggest you take the time to look at the pictures while listening to some of Mozart's music.
The CD on the inside back cover was specifically selected for this book.*

1 IN VIENNA
The Abduction from the Seraglio, K. 384,
overture (excerpt)
Capella Istropolitana conducted by Barry Wordsworth
Naxos CD 8.550185
© + ℗ 1989 HNH INTERNATIONAL LTD.

2 THE DANCER
"German Dance No. 3"
(Three German Dances, K. 605)
Capella Istropolitana conducted by Johannes Wildner
Naxos CD 8.550412
© + ℗ 1990 HNH INTERNATIONAL LTD.

3 FIGARO SEBASTIAN
"Non più andrai," one of Figaro's arias
from *The Marriage of Figaro*, K. 492
*Andrea Martin, baritone; Vienna Mozart Orchestra
conducted by Konrad Leitner*
Naxos CD 8.550867
© 1993 HNH INTERNATIONAL LTD.
℗ 1990 HNH INTERNATIONAL LTD.

4 THE JOURNEY TO ENGLAND
The Marriage of Figaro, K. 492, overture
Capella Istropolitana conducted by Barry Wordsworth
Naxos CD 8.550185
© + ℗ 1989 HNH INTERNATIONAL LTD.

5 ILL IN THE HAGUE
Sonata for Piano in G Major, K. 283, second movement,
Andante (excerpt)
Jenö Jandó, piano
Naxos CD 8.550447
© + ℗ 1991 HNH INTERNATIONAL LTD.

6 Twelve variations on "Ah, vous dirai-je, Maman"
for Organ, K. 265 (excerpt)
Janós Sebestyén, organ
Naxos CD 8.550514
© + ℗ 1991 HNH INTERNATIONAL LTD.

7 THE TWO MOTHERS
Mass in C Major ("Coronation Mass"), K. 618
Camerata Cassovia conducted by Johannes Wildner
Naxos CD 8.550495
© + ℗ 1991 HNH INTERNATIONAL LTD.

8 THE RUINS OF POMPEII
"Deh, vieni alla finestra," one of Don Giovanni's arias
from *Don Giovanni*, K. 527
*Andrea Martin, baritone; Vienna Mozart Orchestra
conducted by Konrad Leitner*
Naxos CD 8.550435
© 1991 HNH INTERNATIONAL LTD.
℗ HNH INTERNATIONAL LTD.

9 CONCERT IN PARIS
Sonata for Piano in C Major, K. 279, first movement,
Allegro (excerpt)
Jenö Jandó, piano
Naxos CD 8.550447
© + ℗ 1991 HNH INTERNATIONAL LTD.

10 THE LIFE THREAD
A Little Night Music, K. 525, first movement,
Allegro (excerpt)
Capella Istropolitana conducted by Wolfgang Sobotka
Naxos CD 8.550026
© 1991 HNH INTERNATIONAL LTD.
℗ 1989 HNH INTERNATIONAL LTD.

11 THE SQUABBLERS
Sonata for Piano in A Major ("Alla Turca"), K. 331
(arranged for orchestra)
Vienna Mozart Orchestra conducted by Konrad Leitner
Naxos CD 8.550866
© 1993 HNH INTERNATIONAL LTD.
℗ 1990 HNH INTERNATIONAL LTD.

12 OPERA IN PRAGUE
Don Giovanni, K. 527, overture
Capella Istropolitana conducted by Barry Wordsworth
Naxos CD 8.550185
© + ℗ HNH INTERNATIONAL LTD.

13 THE SINISTER MESSENGER
Requiem, K. 626, "Dies Irae"
*Choir and orchestra of the Slovak Philharmonic
conducted by Zdendĕk Košler*
Naxos CD 8.550235
© 1991 HNH INTERNATIONAL LTD.
℗ 1986 OPUS RECORDS

14 THE PUPPETEER
"Wie stark ist nicht dein Zauberton,"
one of Tamino's arias from *The Magic Flute*, K. 620
*Herbert Lippert, tenor; Failoni Orchestra
conducted by Michael Halász*
Naxos CD 8.660030
© + ℗ 1994 HNH INTERNATIONAL LTD.

15 "Der Vogelfänger bin ich ja,"
one of Papageno's arias from *The Magic Flute*, K. 620
Georg Tichy, baritone; Failoni Orchestra conducted by Michael Halász
Naxos CD 8.660030
© + ℗ 1994 HNH INTERNATIONAL LTD.

16 "Pa-Pa-Pa," Papageno and Papagena's duet
from *The Magic Flute*, K. 620
*Georg Tichy, baritone; Lotte Leitner, soprano; Failoni Orchestra
conducted by Michael Halász*
Naxos CD 8.660031
© + ℗ 1994 HNH INTERNATIONAL LTD.